My Pet Dog

My Pet Dog

by **Ruth Berman**
photographs by **Billy Hustace**

Lerner Publications Company • Minneapolis

For Andy

Acknowledgments
Thanks go to Sarah and her dog Sadie, Heather and her dog Sam, and Toni and
Pat Yosick, who were photographed for this book. Thanks also to Christie and
Eric Manning, Candice Templeton, Dr. Paul Burton of Benicia Veterinary
Hospital, puppy trainer Kim Osborne, breeder David Eger, and Shirley Trotter
and H. Ramona Rhoads and their Mulburdy Labrador Retrievers for their
contributions to this book.

Additional photos reproduced courtesy of: © Norvia Behling, pp. 11 (both), 13 (upper left, upper right, lower
right, lower left), 14, 18 (left), 24 (lower right), 30 (top, middle right, middle left), 58; © Kent and Donna
Dannen, pp. 13 (middle right), 18 (right), 19, 35 (both); © Alan and Sandy Carey, p. 30 (bottom).

Lerner Publications Company
A division of Lerner Publishing Group
241 First Avenue North
Minneapolis, MN 55401 U.S.A.

Website address: www.lernerbooks.com

Library of Congress Cataloging-in-Publication Data

Berman, Ruth
    My pet dog / by Ruth Berman : photographs by Billy Hustace.
        p.   cm. — (All about pets)
    Includes bibliographical references and index.
    Summary: Text and photographs follow twelve-year-old Cindy as she explains how she chooses and
learns to care for her new Labrador retriever puppy. Also discusses what to consider when selecting a breed
of dog and the general cost of living with a dog.
    ISBN 0-8225-2259-4 (library bdg. : alk. paper)
    1. Dogs—Juvenile literature. [1. Dogs. 2. Pets.] I. Hustace, Billy, ill. II. Title. III. Series
SF426.5.B47   2001
636.7'088'7—dc21   98–50709

Manufactured in the United States of America
1 2 3 4 5 6 — JR — 06 05 04 03 02 01

Contents

I wanted a dog of my very own...

Cinder and I have been friends for nearly a year. Cinder is my dog. I named her Cinder because my name is Cindy. I thought the name Cinder sounded nice with my name.

For as long as I can remember, I've wanted a dog. My parents always said I was too young. "Taking care of a dog is a huge responsibility," my mom would say. "It's not like playing games or playing with your friends. When you're tired, you can't just put away your dog like you can put away your games."

My sister, Tess, and I have fun playing with my dog Cinder.

I helped my friends walk their dogs, and I dreamed about walking my own dog every day.

I spent a lot of time playing with my friends' dogs. But it wasn't the same. I wanted a dog of my very own. Besides, I am *not* too young. I can take care of a dog.

"A dog needs to be walked and trained," my dad would say to me. He asked me if I wouldn't rather have a hamster or a cat. But I wanted to be able to run around and play with my pet. You can't do that with a hamster, and you can't count on a cat wanting to play with you.

"I promise, Dad," I pleaded, "if you let me have a dog, I'll feed it and walk it and train it." That was a week before I was going to be 12.

On my twelfth birthday, my parents surprised me. They gave me a handmade gift certificate for a puppy. "Can we get the puppy now—*please?"* I must have asked that three times before I even let my parents answer.

"First we have to make some decisions," my mom was finally able to say. "We need to decide what kind of dog will fit into our family the best. Then we need to decide where to get our puppy."

Sometimes my mom is *too* responsible. She takes all the fun out of things. But I knew she was right about this. My friend Billy had a dog who didn't fit in with his family. They had to find another home for that dog. Billy's little brother cried for almost a whole week.

I was so excited, I wolfed down my birthday cake after I got my gift certificate for a puppy.

Getting a pet is a family decision. We had to talk—a lot!—about getting a dog before we made up our minds.

We all looked at dog books, and I called my friend to ask her more about her dog.

After school the next day, I went to the library. Dad and my little sister, Tess, came along. We wanted to find out about all the different breeds of dogs and their special traits. When we got home, our whole family got together. We talked about what we wanted and didn't want in a dog. We also talked about what we had to offer a dog.

We knew we needed a dog who would be good with children. Some breeds of dogs just aren't patient enough to live with kids. Some breeds aren't as playful as others. And some breeds become attached to only one or two people. Other breeds think everyone is their friend. Also, we live in the city. We have a yard, but it isn't large enough to give a big dog room to exercise. Then Mom said, "How about getting a mixed breed?"

Mixed breeds come in all sizes. They are every bit as lovable as purebreds!

The books we got from the library explained why it's good to get a purebred dog. You will know the dog's lineage—its parents, grandparents, and so on. That gives you a good idea of what your dog's personality will be like. But my dad reminded us, "Every dog is an individual. So there are personality differences even within breeds."

Tess and I even researched dog breeds with a CD-ROM and on the Internet. There are so many kinds of dogs to choose from, I didn't think I'd ever make up my mind!

Pekingese

What to Consider When Choosing a Breed of Dog

Before you get a dog, you will need to ask yourself and your family some questions. Your answers will help you decide which breed of dog is best for you.

Mixed
Breed
Puppy

- How would I like my dog to look? Think about:
  - long fur vs. short fur (keep in mind that long fur needs more grooming and can be more expensive)
  - pointy nose vs. pushed-up nose (and all the others in between)
  - color
  - curly tail vs. straight tail (or no tail)
  - pointy ears vs. floppy ears
- Do I want a big, medium-sized, or small dog?
- Do I want a slow, quiet dog or a bouncy, active dog?
- Do I want a dog that barks a lot?
- Do I want a dog that is my best friend only or a dog that loves everyone?
- How much room do I have for a dog?
- Do I want a dog that is easy to train or a dog that makes up its own mind?

Bearded
Collie

You probably should get your family together and tally up your answers. When you've decided what you're looking for, browse through some books about dog breeds. Remember, a dog's personality is determined partly by breed. A dog's personality is also shaped by its socialization, or how the dog is treated during its first few months.

Basset
Hound

Boxer

This could be where I get my new puppy...

The weimaraner is one breed that would fit well in our family.

I decided I wanted to get a weimaraner. I first saw one on *Sesame Street* while I was baby-sitting. Two weimaraners were adding and subtracting with balls. They belonged to a photographer named William Wegman. He used these same weimaraners as models for books of fairy tales. Weimaraners are either grayish blue or grayish pink. I think they look really cool.

One of my library books said that weimaraners are good with children. They are affectionate and lively. The book also said they could be stubborn, but I was still interested in this breed. The next step was to find a breeder who raised weimaraners.

I really didn't know where to begin. I thought maybe a pet store would have weimaraners. But my friend Carol told me that many pet stores get their puppies from puppy mills. Puppy mills are places where dogs are raised only to make puppies. The problem is that dogs don't get enough food in these places. They are kept in dirty cages. It's cruel. The dogs often have diseases, and sometimes the puppies aren't formed right.

I wanted to get a healthy puppy whose parents had been treated well. I thought maybe the Humane Society would be able to help. They gave me the phone number of the Purebred Dog Breeders Association. I called them and asked if they knew anyone in my area who bred weimaraners. They did! I called the breeder right away. My heart was pounding. This could be where I get my new puppy!

Finding out about where to get a weimaraner took a lot of calling around.

I was disappointed I didn't find my dog right away. But I was more determined than ever to find the right dog for me.

But 10 minutes later, I was ready to cry. The breeder was really nice, but she said that her weimaraners cost $750 each. I knew that was more money than my parents would spend on my birthday gift. The breeder also said that many people aren't happy with weimaraners. They need a lot of exercise and attention.

I figured that any purebred dog would be pretty expensive. I had to think everything over again. Puppies at the Humane Society weren't nearly as expensive as puppies from breeders. But I really wanted to meet my puppy's parents. Then I would be able to tell more about my dog's personality. "Back to the books," I thought. Weimaraners are hunting dogs. Maybe other hunting dogs wouldn't be as expensive.

When puppies are this young, they have to stay with their mother.

Labrador retrievers! They're great dogs, too. They're good with kids, and they're big enough but not too big. I found the number of a breeder, but she said her dogs cost $300 each. That was still a lot of money.

I guess I must have sounded pretty disappointed, because the breeder told me to hold the line for a moment. A few minutes later, she said she had some good news for me. One of her dogs had been bred as part of a 4-H project. Only four of the puppies were spoken for. If I was interested, I could reserve a puppy for $100. The puppies would be born in about two weeks. They would be ready to leave their mother in about 10 weeks. Hooray!

Smaller dogs generally cost less to feed than larger dogs, but all dogs need shots and toys.

I talked to my family about these puppies. Everyone was really excited. But my mom said that we also had to consider other costs. Puppies need shots, food, and other things. I already had $80 saved up. So we agreed that I would help pay for the shots.

Quickly, I called the breeder back. Boy, just when I thought getting this puppy was a done deal! The breeder told me she had some questions for me. I had to answer them before she would let me buy one of her puppies.

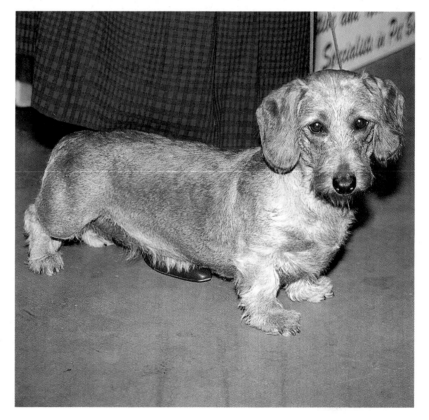

The questions weren't hard, though. My family and I had already discussed most of them. I felt really proud that I had done my homework. I knew I was ready to say yes, I want one of those puppies!

Labs come in three colors. I didn't care if my puppy was going to be yellow, chocolate, or black. But I did want a female, mainly because *I'm* a girl. I was the third person in line for a female. It was finally time to get the house ready for a puppy!

I liked all three kinds of Labs—black, yellow, and even chocolate!

General Cost of Living with a Dog

Taking care of a dog can cost a lot of money. Here is a list of some of the costs, which will vary depending on where you live.

- **Medical costs**
  - Shots for the first year: $200
  - Shots after the first year: $65 a year
  - General care: $35 a year
  - Flea and tick care: $80 a year

- **Feeding a dog**
  - Depending on size: $160-$400 a year

- **Toys and grooming supplies**
  - Toys: $50-$200 a year
  - One visit to the groomer: $50

- **Boarding**
  - A two-week stay: $300

- **Obedience school**
  - For the first year: $50-$100
  - For advanced training: $50-$200

Add up the yearly costs. You will see that one year of care for one dog can cost more than $1,000. Before you decide to get a dog, be sure you will be able to give your dog everything it will need.

Information courtesy of the Humane Society of the United States

I kept my fingers crossed all week long...

There are so many different ways to go about raising a puppy! I had to choose a way that would match my family's lifestyle. First, we decided to buy a kennel, so the puppy would have a special place of her own. We would put the puppy in the kennel at night and when we would all leave the house. That way, she wouldn't be able to chew things up or have accidents all over the house. At other times, I would just keep my eye on her.

At first I thought putting my puppy in a kennel would be mean. But then I remembered I had read that dogs like covered spaces. Their wolf ancestors live in dens. Dens make dogs feel safe and secure.

Puppies feel comfortable and safe in a kennel.

Mom thought it was a good idea to put away her vases. I hid cords that could be dangerous for a puppy.

I needed to puppy-proof the house too. I crawled around and pretended I was a puppy. Anything I thought could be dangerous I moved to a higher place. I hid electrical cords and asked Mom to put away her glass vases. I didn't want her to be mad at my new puppy if the pup accidentally broke something.

Then I had to decide where my puppy would sleep. I wanted her to sleep in bed with me, but my parents said no way! "That's half the fun of having a puppy of my very own," I complained. But the answer was still no. So I decided to move the kennel into my room at night.

Puppies need a few things right away when they come to a new home. They need bowls for food and water and a few toys. Everyone wanted to get ready for the puppy. So the whole family climbed into the car and went to the pet store.

We looked at the dog dishes first. There were so many different kinds! There were plastic, ceramic, and metal bowls. They came in lots of different sizes, colors, and designs.

Mom and I were overwhelmed with all the things we could buy for our new puppy. The dog beds looked so soft and comfortable, I wanted to take a nap in one.

The toys were next. There were stuffed toys, fake bones, string toys, plastic squeaky toys, rawhides. . . . I could go on and on!

The guy at the pet store told me that it's not a good idea to buy your dog lots of toys. A dog with too many toys will have a hard time figuring out what a toy is and what things are important to people. He also told me not to let my puppy chew on an old shoe. If you let your puppy chew on an old shoe, she will think it's okay to chew on a new shoe, too. He said the same rule applies to socks.

If puppies have toys to play with, they won't chew on your stuff as much.

Playing with your dog is an important part of each day for both you and your dog. I couldn't wait to have my own dog to play with!

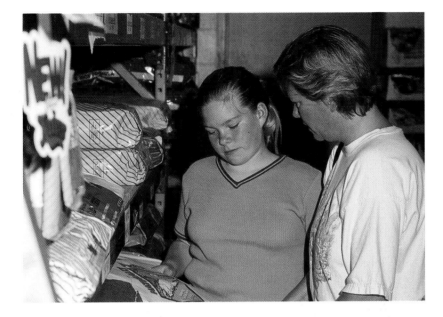

After looking at bags of dog food, we decided to ask the breeder what the puppies had already been eating.

Then he warned me to be careful about a toy's size. "Dogs can choke to death on toys that are small enough to go down their throat," he said. So I ended up buying a hard fake bone, a ball, and a squeaky stuffed toy. They were all big enough that my puppy wouldn't choke on them. They were also small enough that she could carry them around.

Then I had to figure out what to feed my new puppy. The guy at the pet store said to check with my veterinarian—that's an animal doctor—to find out what food he or she recommends. He also suggested that I find out what my breeder fed the puppies. It's a good idea to feed dogs the food they are used to. If you have to change their food, change it slowly. Otherwise, it might upset their stomach. So I decided to wait and talk to the breeder.

After calling around, I found a puppy kindergarten where I could learn how to train my puppy.

When we got home from the pet store, I checked out obedience schools. I wanted to take my dog to obedience school as soon as possible. I called all the schools that were close to where I live. I wanted to find out how much they cost and what age a puppy should be to start. I also wanted to know what kind of training they used. There seem to be as many kinds of training as there are puppy toys!

Many places said I had to wait for my puppy to be six months old before enrolling her in school. But I found a few places that had puppy kindergartens. Puppies in kindergarten could be as young as seven weeks old. I chose a school and signed up my puppy for classes.

Days and days went by. Finally, the call came. My puppy had been born! I was ready to go get her right away. The breeder reminded me that I had to wait at least seven weeks. "Seven weeks?!" It was already two months past my birthday, and I still didn't have my puppy. But the breeder let me set up a time to visit the puppies when they would be a few weeks old. That way I could meet my puppy's parents, too.

I was scared, because if I didn't like the parents, I'd be disappointed. I'd have to start looking for a puppy all over again. I didn't want to do that.

The breeder gave me a picture of one of the puppies in the litter when they were just a few weeks old.

The breeder was a long way out of town. But maybe it just seemed that way because I was so excited. When we finally got there, I couldn't believe it! There were so many dogs—and they were all Labs!

Since this was going to be my dog, I was the one who had to talk to the breeder. I told her who I was and what I wanted. She told me what kind of food she feeds her dogs. She said that when I picked up my new puppy in a few weeks, she would tell me how much to feed her and anything else I needed to know.

The breeder answered all my questions. I don't know how she could give up such cute puppies!

Then we saw Sadie—my puppy's mother—and all her puppies. I had never seen such cute puppies! They were all golden yellow. Sadie looked really tired, but she was sweet and well trained. I knew right away that I had made the right decision. Everyone else in my family liked Sadie a lot too.

I wanted to take my puppy home right then! But I knew that there are stages every puppy goes through. Puppies need their mother and littermates to help them get through the first seven or eight weeks. So I waited.

The puppies looked so much alike. I didn't know how I'd be able to choose just one.

Socialization and the First Stages of a Puppy's Life

Puppies are especially quick learners during the first 16 weeks of their lives. They learn the right and wrong ways to act with other dogs. They learn to accept new situations. And they learn to enjoy being with people.

Socializing a puppy means introducing a puppy to new things to shape its behavior.

From birth to three weeks of age, puppies need their mother, their littermates, and a clean area. Puppies at this stage who are picked up and petted by people will handle stress better when they are adult dogs. They may also be friendlier than dogs who don't receive this kind of socialization.

Four-week-old puppies begin to explore beyond their "dens" and littermates. By five weeks of age, puppies should be exposed to new experiences, such as a variety of floor surfaces, sounds, and objects. Six-week-old puppies start to seek attention from people.

During their sixth and seventh weeks, puppies learn manners from their mother and littermates. For example, puppies learn when to bite and when not to bite.

Because puppies learn from their families, they should not be taken away from them too soon. It's best to wait until your puppy is seven weeks old before you bring it home.

This puppy was just right...

The day had finally come to bring my puppy home. The whole family piled into the car and off we went. This time it seemed to take even longer for us to get to the breeder's. Everyone was excited. Tess sang, "How much is that doggy in the window. . . . " Mom and Dad whistled along. I stared out the window, craning my neck to see the final turnoff to the breeder's place.

"We're here!" I shouted as I leapt out of the car. The moment my feet touched the ground, I ran to see the puppies. But they weren't in the kennel. "There they are!" I shouted to my family.

I wanted to pet the puppies as soon as I saw them.

The puppies' mother was watching and sniffing them with her forehead all wrinkled up. I think she was a little worried. But she was okay enough to lick my hand when I went over to pet her.

Then it struck me. Out of all these cute, wiggly, grunting, squealing, soft little critters, I had to pick ONE. How was I going to pick just one? I knew I was in trouble.

Just then the breeder came out of the office. We talked for a minute, then she said, "I have a few questions that will help you pick your puppy." Phew! I relaxed knowing I was going to get some help.

Sadie and her puppies played more with each other than with their toys.

Because the puppies had been socialized, they warmed up to me right away.

The breeder said that she had socialized the puppies. That's why they were in the house instead of the kennel. "What does *socialized* mean?" I asked.

"These puppies have lived outside and played and slept inside. They have played with children of all ages. They have been around cars and trucks, vacuum cleaners, and hair dryers," she explained. She said that if puppies aren't well socialized, they will freak out at every new situation.

A male puppy yanked on his sister's tail. He was dominant and independent— not my kind of puppy.

"They're just starting to wake up from a nap," the breeder said. "See that puppy over there? See how he always has to be first and how he likes to pull on anything he can get his teeth on? He's going to be a handful! Many breeders would call this puppy the pick of the litter. He is the biggest, most independent puppy of the litter. But this kind of puppy is not everyone's idea of the best pet."

The other two people who were ahead of me to choose a female had already come and gone. There were four females left. The others were males. One by one, I picked up a puppy and walked out of sight of the other puppies. I could tell that two of the females were just like that male. They were going to be a handful!

Dogs as Pack Animals

Alaskan Malamute

The wolf is considered to be the dog's ancestor. Wolves are pack animals, which means they live in groups. Your dog has the instinct to develop packs the way wolves do. If you learn about wolf-pack behavior, you will learn more about your dog.

Each wolf in a pack holds its own position, or rank, in the pack. We call the top wolf the alpha wolf. Each pack has an alpha male wolf and an alpha female wolf. They are the parents of most all of the other wolves in the pack.

The alpha pair maintain their dominance, or their high rank, through their behavior. The alpha male leads the way down a narrow path, and the alpha female is next in line. The alpha wolves eat first. Alpha wolves mate and produce young. The other wolves help raise and feed the young.

Dominant wolves hold themselves taller than lower-ranked wolves that are subordinate. A dominant wolf holds its tail stiff and upright. Other wolves in the pack hold their tails straight out or down or between their legs. Dominant wolves often place their heads on top of a subordinate's shoulders. A subordinate wolf greets a dominant wolf by licking him or her on the chin.

If you want to learn more, you can read books and take your dog to obedience training school. You can learn how to use "wolf-pack language" with your dog.

Wolf (Canis lupus)

Another female was practically the opposite. She kept rolling over on her back, and urine would trickle out. At first I thought that was funny. Then the breeder explained that this puppy was submissive. "The other puppies are dominant," the breeder said. "They would like nothing better than to be king of the puppies. But this puppy is the opposite. She would rather give up than fight."

The breeder said that this submissive puppy wouldn't be as happy with children. She would be better off in a quiet home with a gentle person.

The breeder's assistant agreed that this puppy would be too submissive for our home.

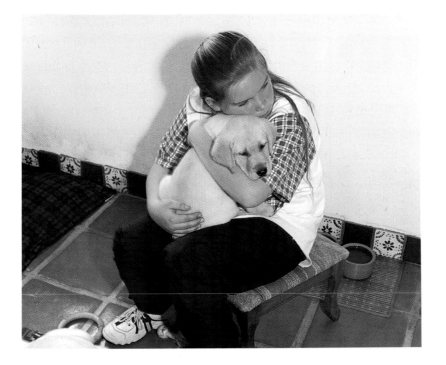

When I hugged Cinder, I knew she was perfect for me and our family.

We were down to the last female. She was a little shy at first, but then she sniffed me and started to dart around. I got up and ran, and she followed! That made me feel special, but the breeder said that all puppies that age follow leaders. Anyway, she didn't roll over on her back all the time. My dad and I checked her over to make sure she looked healthy. We made sure that her eyes were clear. We made sure that there were no bad smells coming out of her ears or mouth. She looked and smelled fine.

"SHE'S BEAUTIFUL! I LOVE HER! SHE'S MY PUPPY!" I couldn't believe it. I knew right away I wanted to name her Cinder.

Cinder cried a little when we started off in the car. Actually, it sounded more like whimpering and grunting. But she snuggled down into the box we had brought for her. After a while she fell asleep. So did I. I guess we were both tired out from all the excitement.

Cinder wasn't too nervous to sleep on the ride home.

Cinder sniffed every room. I followed her to make sure we had puppy-proofed the house well enough.

When we got home, I put Cinder in the living room and just watched her explore. She sniffed around and seemed a little scared, but she sure was curious. Once or twice, she started to cry. Then I said her name, and she bounded over to me. I don't think she knew her name yet, but I think she liked hearing my voice.

When I saw Cinder sniffing around in a circle, I quickly and gently picked her up and took her outside. The breeder had said to watch for that. Sniffing and circling is a sure sign that a puppy needs to go outside.

The breeder said, "When you are housetraining your dog, it's important not to let your puppy have an accident. And it's important to always be consistent." She said if Cinder had an accident in the house, I should quietly and gently take her out of the room. Then I should clean up the mess. I had to make sure Cinder couldn't smell her accident there.

My plan was to take Cinder outside every time she woke up, finished eating or drinking, and stopped playing. Sometimes I forgot my plan during our first few days together.

When we were outside, Cinder was more interested in exploring the yard than doing her business. It was a nice day, so I decided to just stay outside for a while. I wanted to wait until Cinder did her business so I could praise her. She finally did, and I told her what a good puppy she was.

Cinder ran through the flowers when I took her outside.

CHAPTER 5

I wanted to take Cinder everywhere...

Cinder liked her dog food and gobbled it down.

I looked at my watch and saw that two hours had passed since we got home. It was time to feed Cinder. I measured out the food the way the breeder had shown me. Cinder wolfed it down! She ate so fast I thought she was going to be sick—but she wasn't. She had just gone outside, but I took her outside again—just in case. Puppies are supposed to need to do their business right after they eat. So I took her out, and sure enough. . . . I praised Cinder again for a job well done.

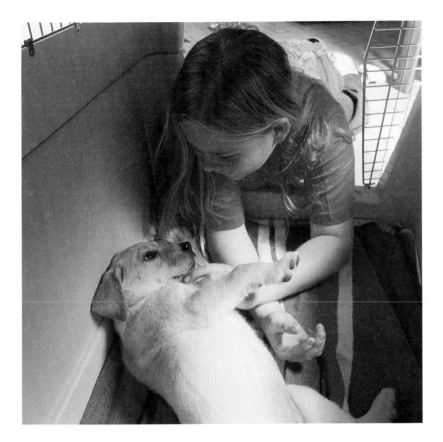

Cinder got used to her kennel right away.

Then I could tell Cinder was really tired, so I took her to my bedroom. I showed her the kennel. She walked right in! I hopped into bed myself, but I wanted to read, not sleep.

Cinder slept for over an hour. Actually, even though I wanted to read, I fell asleep too. I thought there was a siren in my dream, but it really was Cinder crying. I told her she was a good girl to come right to me after she woke up. Then I took her right out the door to the yard. Cinder got praised again for doing her business.

Everything went well that first day. Tess played with Cinder for a while until we had dinner. I fed Cinder again, and my friend Carol came over to see her.

Then it was night. A couple hours before bedtime, I took Cinder's water away. I let her outside again right before I went to sleep. That first day, Cinder had no accidents—she was the perfect puppy. But my luck ran out.

All of a sudden, I had a demon dog. Cinder just wouldn't settle down in her kennel for the night. She cried and whimpered and wailed. She pawed at my bed, but I just ignored her. Finally, she quieted down. I think we both fell asleep at about the same time.

Cinder loves it when Carol and I rub her stomach.

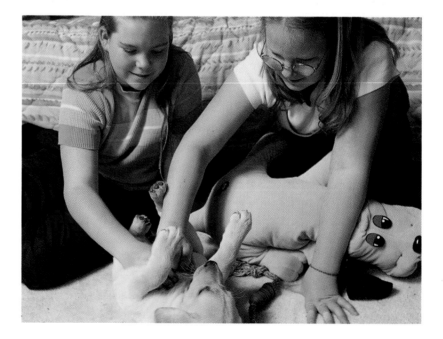

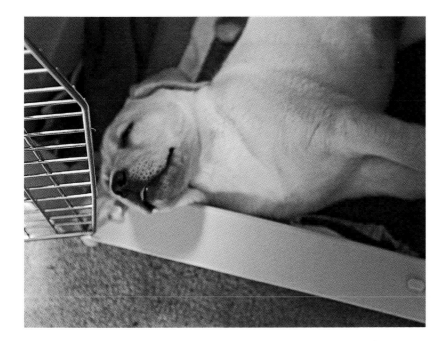

Cinder slept well in her kennel—for a while, that is. Letting Cinder out during the night got tiring sometimes.

I knew Cinder would need to relieve herself a couple times during the night. Some time in the night, I heard Cinder moving around. I woke up and stumbled outside with her. I was right. That's what she had to do. Then she wanted to play. Oh brother! When she figured out that I wouldn't play with her, she started to cry again. When we were back inside, I gave her a toy to chew on, and that kept her quiet. Then she must have fallen asleep.

The next thing I knew, it was morning. Okay, it was four in the morning, but Cinder hadn't had an accident. I took her outside again, then back to bed. She cried a little, then went back to sleep. We had made it through our first night together. Every night was like this for the first few weeks.

I wanted Cinder to get used to different experiences, like climbing stairs.

I wanted to take Cinder everywhere I went. From my reading, I had learned that during the first few weeks I should let Cinder have as many experiences as possible. I also knew that at 8 weeks old and at 11 weeks old, Cinder would go through a fear period. If anything scared her during that time, she might be afraid of it for the rest of her life. So I wanted to try to do a lot with her that first week.

I helped her learn to walk up the stairs. I wanted to build her confidence, and I wanted her to be able to get to my room whenever she wanted. At first she looked all wobbly and funny. But she took to it right away!

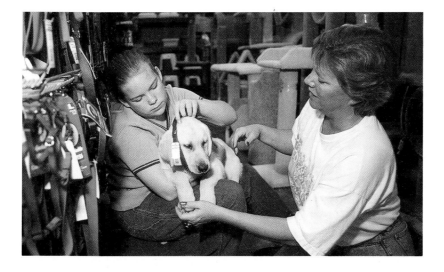

Mom and I tried a bunch of collars on Cinder before finding the right one. Cinder had a hard time walking with a leash and collar at first.

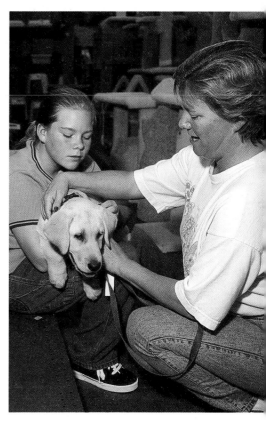

One day, I decided to take Cinder to the pet store to buy her a leash and collar. We chose a collar that we could adjust. That way she wouldn't grow out of it right away.

I chose a leash that matched. I decided to get a cotton web leash because it didn't hurt my hand when my mom pulled the other end. This leash was also lightweight and had a small snap, so it wouldn't be too heavy for Cinder.

Once we had chosen Cinder's "outfit," I decided to walk her on the leash. Hah! I guess what I thought and what Cinder thought were two different things. She wiggled and tossed her little self all over, trying to get that collar off. I just kept telling her she was a good girl. I was afraid that if I yelled at her to behave, she might learn to hate the leash and collar. I let her lead me to wherever she wanted to go.

Tess and Cinder took a nap together in Cinder's kennel.

Another day after lunch, I fed Cinder and then I had to do some chores. Cinder slept while I cleaned up the kitchen. When I was done, I went to check on her. Tess had crawled into Cinder's bed and they were sleeping together. They looked so cute! I ran and got Mom and Dad, but by the time Dad had found his camera, Cinder and Tess were looking up at us all bleary-eyed and confused. I asked Tess if she wanted to go for a walk with Cinder and me.

Cinder fought her collar and leash a little. She got interested in the new smells of the sidewalks and lawns. I let her wander around and didn't worry about her pulling or anything. I just wanted her to have fun with Tess and me, and I wanted Tess and me to have fun with her. And we did.

The day came that we had to take Cinder to the vet. I had decided to take Cinder to the vet that my friend Billy and his family go to, because they like him so much. I was still nervous. I guess I was scared that the vet would find something wrong. Then we might have to take Cinder back.

First the vet weighed her. Then he checked Cinder's ears and eyes. He took Cinder's temperature and listened to her heart. It was a lot like when I go to the doctor. Cinder even had to have a shot. I thought she would cry, but she didn't even stop wagging her tail! She kept licking the vet's face, too.

Cinder didn't even feel it when the vet gave her a shot. I was more nervous than she was!

The vet told me that dogs don't get fat and lazy because of being spayed or neutered. The operation is important to a dog's health, unless you want your dog to have puppies.

The vet said that Cinder was a very healthy puppy, but she had worms. "Yuck!" I thought. But the vet said that almost every puppy has worms. All I had to do was give Cinder some pills for a few days. The vet showed me how. Then he told me when I had to bring Cinder back for more shots. He also talked to me about having her spayed so she couldn't have puppies.

Spaying and neutering are important operations. If male dogs are not neutered, they can go wild around female dogs. If female dogs are not spayed, they get messy and have to wear something like a diaper when they go into heat. That happens about twice a year. Plus, a female dog who never gets spayed has a greater chance of getting mammary cancer. So I decided that when Cinder turned six months old, I would have her spayed. I had to start saving money for that right away.

Then I thought the vet was kidding around with me. He said that I should start brushing Cinder's teeth! He gave me a toothbrush, made especially for dogs, and meat-flavored toothpaste. I thought the idea of brushing Cinder's teeth was really silly. But the vet said it would save me money in the future. If Cinder ever has to have her teeth cleaned, she will have to be given an anesthetic, which is expensive. If I brush Cinder's teeth, she won't have to have her teeth cleaned by the vet so often. Okay. I bought the toothbrush and toothpaste too.

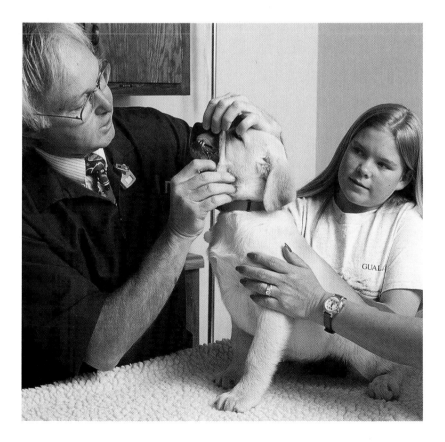

Brushing your dog's teeth is good for her health, just like brushing your teeth is good for you. Cinder loves the meat-flavored toothpaste we got from the vet.

Shaping Your Puppy's Behavior

To have an obedient dog, all the people in your family should hold a dominant position in your puppy's pack. Here are some easy things you can do every day to remind your puppy that you are the alpha dog.

- Have your puppy sit before eating, going outside, getting petted, or getting a treat. Teaching your puppy the basic commands of *sit, down, stay,* and *come* will help you keep the top dog position.

- Be sure you always go through a door or down a narrow path ahead of your puppy.

- When you scold a puppy, you may be encouraging the bad behavior. It's best to ignore the pup's naughty behavior and distract her. You can clap your hands once or twice or shake a tin can filled with marbles. Then try to get her to do something that's okay, like playing with a dog toy. Always praise your puppy as soon as she is being good. Be consistent and . . . **NEVER EVER** hit or scream at your puppy!

- There is another way to discipline your puppy when catching him or her in the act of being naughty. Grab the pup by the scruff (under his ear) and gently shake. This is called the scruff shake. Dogs discipline each other this way all the time.

- If your pup is jumping or chewing on you, try to ignore her for a minute or two. Turn your back, close your eyes, and keep your arms close to your body. This will make your puppy feel cut off from you. As soon as your puppy has calmed down, quietly praise her.

I have the smartest dog in the world...

During the next couple of weeks, Cinder and I just played and played. Tess and Cinder played a lot too. I tried to get Cinder used to words like *come, stay, treat,* and *outside.* But I never played tug-of-war with her. Pulling and tugging on a dog's toy can make the dog mean. Also, if I played rough with Cinder, she didn't know when to stop. She would nip me. So when I wanted to go wild with Cinder, we played fetch or tag.

Tess and I played with Cinder after she came to me when I called her.

When Cinder was about nine weeks old, we started obedience school. I had picked a school that hardly ever uses the word "no" to train dogs. Instead, they ignore naughty dogs or praise good dogs. They also use a special training collar that I had never seen before. It is like a head halter. The trainer said the straps of the halter gently press on certain areas called dominance spots. Those are the spots mother dogs use to discipline their puppies. You know how, when a puppy is bad, the mother puts her open mouth over the puppy's nose? That's a dominance spot.

The first evening was a mess, but it was a blast too. Puppies, puppies everywhere! They were all so different and so cute. They were all jumping and barking and yanking on their leashes.

Puppy kindergarten was filled with all different kinds of puppies. Tess and I learned how to teach Cinder to understand our commands.

Cinder's buckle collar was checked for size, and I decided to buy a 10-foot leash. My instructor said that I should attach one end of the leash to me and the other end to Cinder. That way, I would know if Cinder started doing anything bad. Then I could correct her right away. I could pull on the leash or quickly take her outside. This was a good way to keep my eye on Cinder while I was doing chores or other things.

Cinder did really well because we had been training at home. By the end of our 10-week class, Cinder knew all the basic commands.

All my friends love to play with Cinder, especially since she's well trained.

Day after day and week after week, Cinder and I played. Sometimes we played by ourselves. Other times we played with Tess, Carol, or Billy. Mom and Dad liked to play too, and Tess loved throwing sticks for Cinder.

Day after day and week after week, Cinder and I trained too. We only trained about 10 or 15 minutes at a time. Sometimes, even though it was such a short amount of time, I'd get fed up with Cinder. Then I would just stop training. But sometimes I thought she was the smartest dog in the world. She seemed to learn things even if I was goofing up the lesson.

Even after puppy kindergarten, Cinder and I still learn how to get along better every day. Cleaning up after Cinder during walks isn't fun, but we want to be good neighbors.

Finally, the 10-week puppy kindergarten was over. Even though we had already learned a lot, Cinder and I have continued training at the obedience school. Every day we learn even more about how to get along with each other.

Mom, Dad, and Tess have been learning too. Everyone has made mistakes. Once I yelled at Cinder for digging holes in Mom's garden. First of all, I shouldn't have yelled at Cinder, because I didn't catch her in the act. She couldn't understand why I was so angry. But worst of all, my mom had dug the holes! Oops. Luckily, Cinder has forgiven me.

Have Fun with Your Dog

Taking your puppy to obedience school is a good idea for many reasons. Your dog will grow up with good manners and will become socialized. Best of all, you can join in the activities and competitions designed for dogs. Here are some fun games you can play with your dog:

Agility: An obstacle course is set up with items such as see-saws, tunnels, hoop jumps, and weave poles. You guide your dog to run through this course as fast and as precisely as possible. The fastest dog with the fewest mistakes wins.

Flyball: Flyball is a relay race between teams of four dogs of any size or breed. One dog from each team races across the course, jumping over four hurdles. At the end of the course is a box with a spring-loaded lever. The dog steps on the lever, sending a tennis ball into the air. The dog catches the ball and races back down the course, jumping over the hurdles. Then the next dog takes off. The first team to have all four dogs run without errors wins! Your dog must be well trained before you try this game.

Frisbee: When you and your dog get good at playing Frisbee, you can enter Frisbee competitions, like the Toss-Fetch. Person/dog teams have 60 seconds to complete as many throws and catches as possible. The longer the throw, the higher the score. The game Freestyle is a timed routine set to music, with routines that include throws and tricks.

Talk to people at your obedience school and go to dog shows. You'll find out more ways to have fun with your four-legged friend!

Since I've had Cinder, I've learned that having a dog is a lot of hard work. It's an important responsibility. Sometimes it's scary, sometimes it's nerve-racking, and sometimes it's maddening. But all mixed up with that is the fun, silliness, friendship, and love that Cinder and I have for each other.

I can see that all the waiting and preparing paid off. If I hadn't done all those things, I don't know if I would have ended up with the right pet for me. I just wish everyone would think hard before getting a dog, so everyone could be as happy with their dog as I am with Cinder.

Cinder has really become my best friend!

Glossary

4-H: a program set up by the U.S. Department of Agriculture to teach young people useful skills about farming, animal breeding, and carpentry. The number "4" refers to head, heart, hands, and health.

Breeder: a person who breeds animals

Breeds: groups of animals that are related and have similar characteristics

Housetraining: housebreaking. Training a pet to live indoors and go to the "toilet" outside

Instinct: (*in*-stingkt): a way of feeling or acting that is natural to an animal, rather than learned

Littermates: offspring from the same group, or litter, of animals born to one mother. The mother gives birth to her babies at one time.

Mammary cancer (*mam*-uh-ree *kan*-sur): cancer of the mammary glands in the breasts

Neuter: (*noo*-ter): to remove the sex organs (testicles) from a male animal so that it is unable to reproduce

Purebred: an animal bred from members of a recognized breed, or kind of animal, without mixing in other animals' blood

Rawhides: cattle skin hardened and shaped like bones for dogs to chew on

Traits: inherited characteristics. Qualities that make a person or animal special

Socialization: the shaping of a young animal's behavior by exposing it to people and a variety of experiences

Spay: to remove the sex organs (uterus and ovaries) from a female animal so that it is unable to reproduce

Resources

American Animal Hospital Association
http://www.healthypet.com

American Boarding Kennels Association
4575 Galley Rd., Ste. 400A
Colorado Springs, CO 80915
http://www.abka.com

American Kennel Club
5580 Centerview Dr., Ste. 200
Raleigh, NC 27606
919/233-9767
http://www.akc.org

American Veterinary Medical Association
http://www.avma.org

Animal Network
http://www.animalnetwork.com/default.asp

National Dog Owners Association
PO Box 8166
Reston, VA 20195
http://www.dogowners.org/public/files/welcome.html

For Further Reading

American Kennel Club, The. *American Kennel Club Dog Care and Training.* New York: Howell Book House, 1991.

American Kennel Club, The. *The Complete Dog Book for Kids.* New York: Howell Book House, 1996.

Byars, Betsy. *Tornado.* New York: HarperCollins Publishers, 1996.

Cleary, Beverly. *Strider.* New York: Morrow Junior Books, 1991.

Cutler, Jane. *No Dogs Allowed.* New York: Farrar Straus Giroux, 1992.

Gardner, J. R. *Housebreaking and Training Puppies: A Complete Up-To-Date Guide (Basic Domestic Pet Library).* Philadelphia: Chelsea House Publishers (Library), 1997.

Hesse, Karen. *Sable.* New York: Henry Holt and Company, 1994.

Johnson, Sylvia A., and Alice Aamodt. *Wolf Pack: Tracking Wolves in the Wild.* Minneapolis: Lerner, 1985.

Patent, Dorothy Hinshaw. *Dogs: The Wolf Within.* Minneapolis: Carolrhoda, 1993.

Rock, Maxine A. *Totally Fun Things To Do With Your Dog (Play With Your Pet).* New York: John Wiley and Sons, 1998.

Rosen, Michael J. *Kids' Best Dog Book.* New York: Workman Publishing, 1993.

Snow, Alan. *How Dogs Really Work!* Boston, Toronto, and London: Little, Brown, 1993.

Index

ABOUT THE AUTHOR

Ruth Berman was born in New York and grew up in Minnesota. As a child, she spent her time going to school and saving lost and hurt animals. Later, Ruth volunteered at three zoos and got her degree in English. She enjoys writing science books for children. She has written six books in Lerner's Pull Ahead series. Her other books include *Ants* and *Peacocks* (Lerner Publications) and *Sharks* and *American Bison* (Carolrhoda Books). Ruth lives in California with her husband, Andy, her dogs Hannah and Baxter, and her cats, Nikki and Toby.

ABOUT THE PHOTOGRAPHER

Billy Hustace is a widely published photographer whose work has appeared in magazines including *National Geographic World*, *Dog World*, *Dog Fancy*, and the *New York Times Sunday Magazine.* He is a graduate of Temple University in Philadelphia, and he lives in Oakland, California, with his family.